Sam Smith
EASY PIANO COLLECTION

ISBN 978-1-70513-108-4

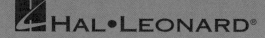

HAL•LEONARD®

Visit Hal Leonard Online at
www.halleonard.com

Contact us:
Hal Leonard
7777 West Bluemound Road
Milwaukee, WI 53213
Email: info@halleonard.com

In Europe, contact:
Hal Leonard Europe Limited
42 Wigmore Street
Marylebone, London, W1U 2RN
Email: info@halleonardeurope.com

In Australia, contact:
Hal Leonard Australia Pty. Ltd.
4 Lentara Court
Cheltenham, Victoria, 3192 Australia
Email: info@halleonard.com.au

DANCING WITH A STRANGER

Words and Music by SAM SMITH,
TOR HERMANSEN, MIKKEL ERIKSEN,
NORMANI HAMILTON and JAMES NAPIER

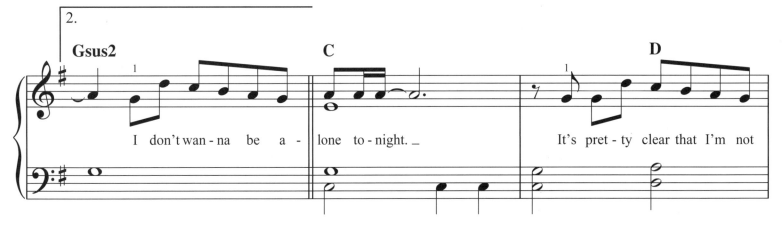

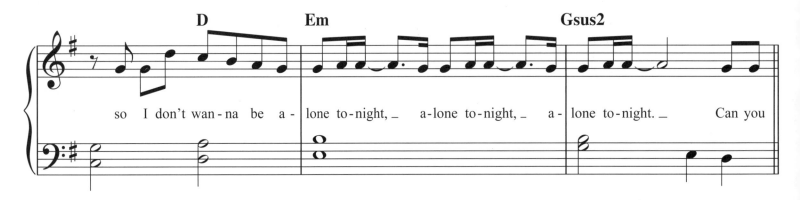

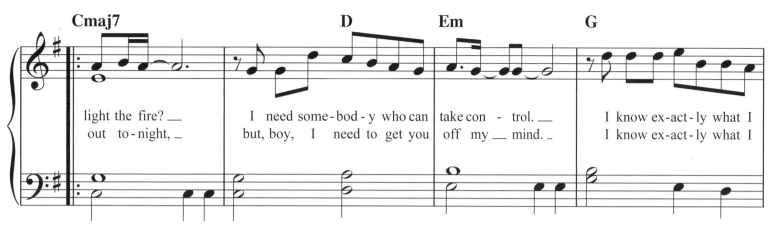

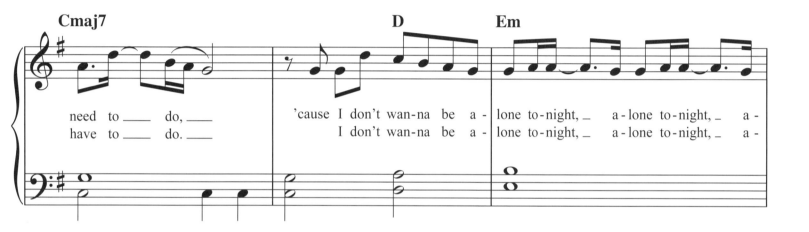

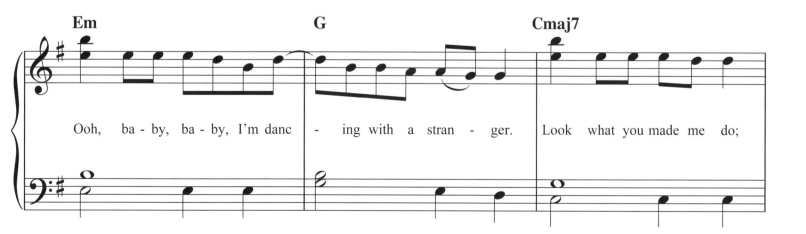

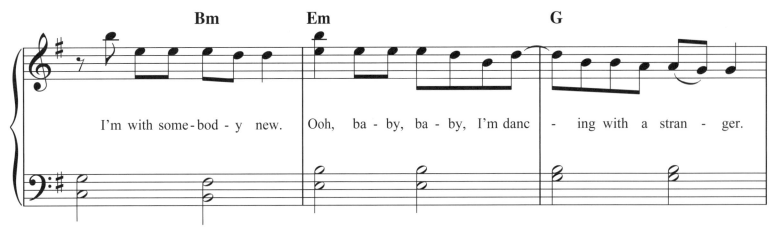

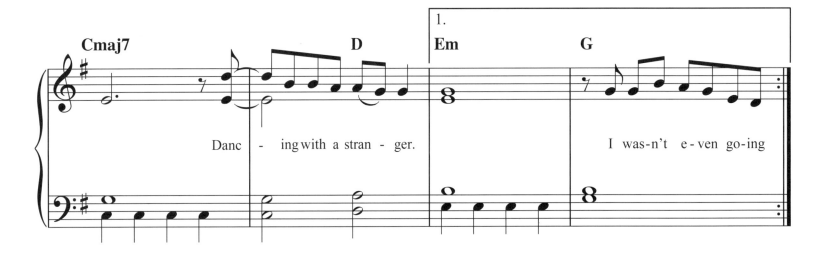

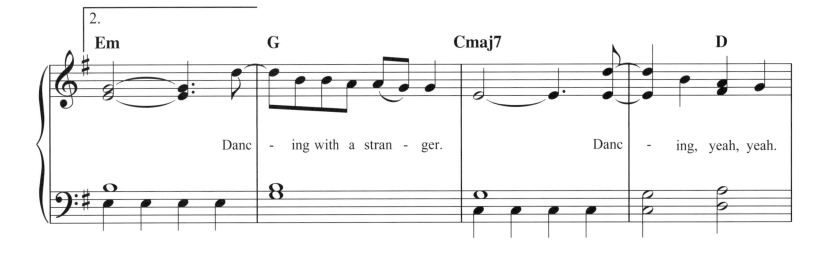

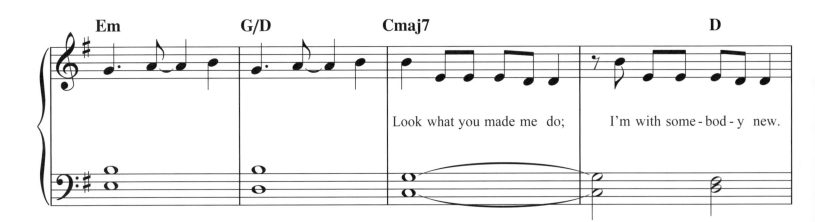

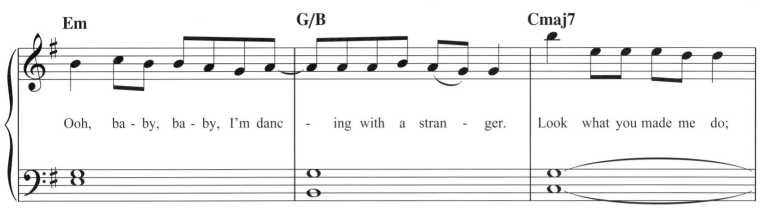

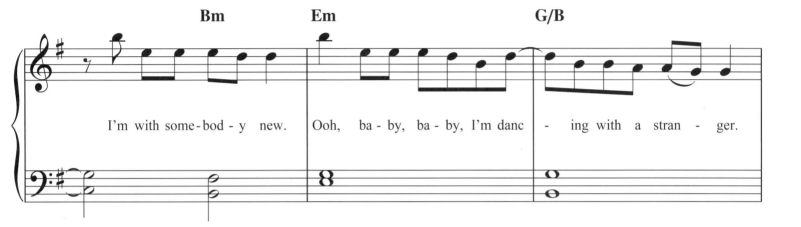

DIAMONDS

Words and Music by SAM SMITH,
OSCAR GORRES and SHELLBACK

Moderately fast

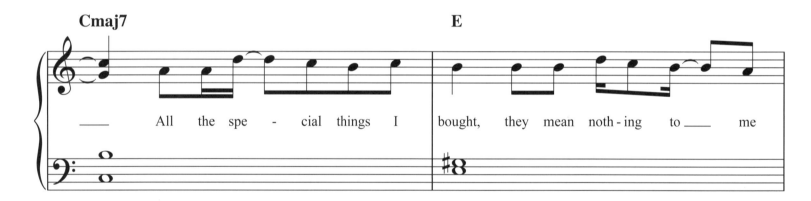

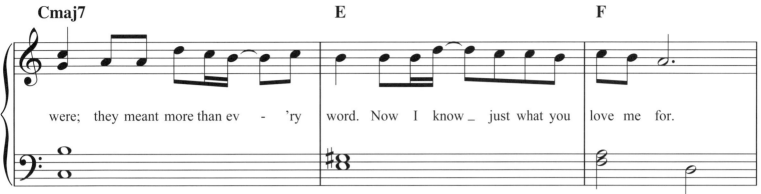

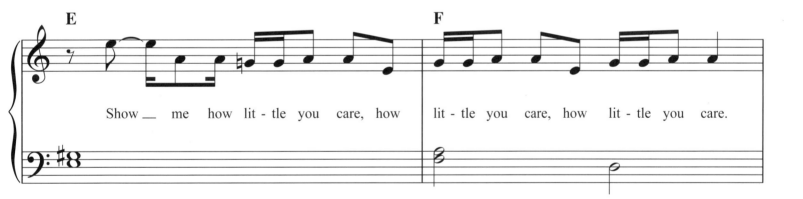

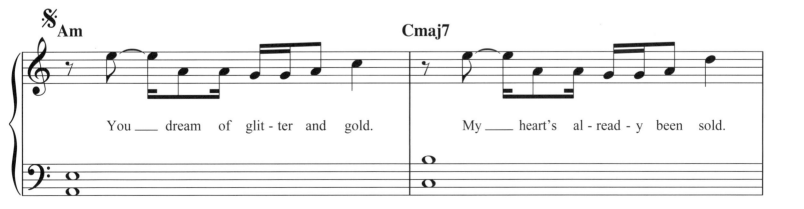

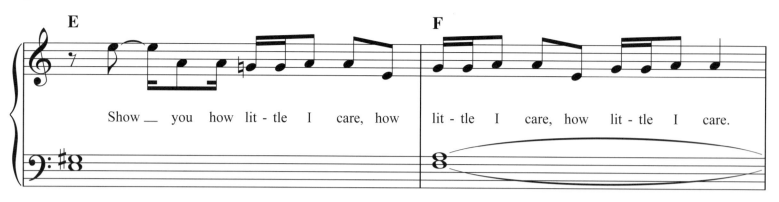

Show — you how lit - tle I care, how lit - tle I care, how lit - tle I care.

My dia-monds leave with you. You're nev-er gon-na hear my heart break, — nev-er gon-na move in

dark ways. — Ba - by, you're so cruel. My dia-monds leave with you. Ma - te - ri - al love won't

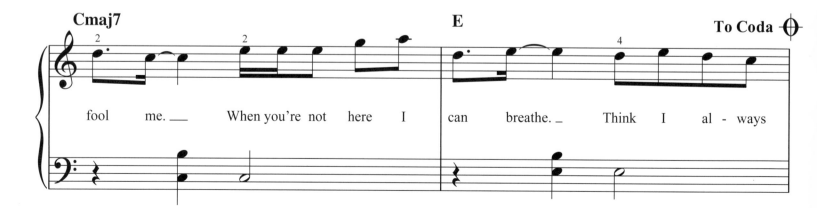

fool me. — When you're not here I can breathe. — Think I al - ways

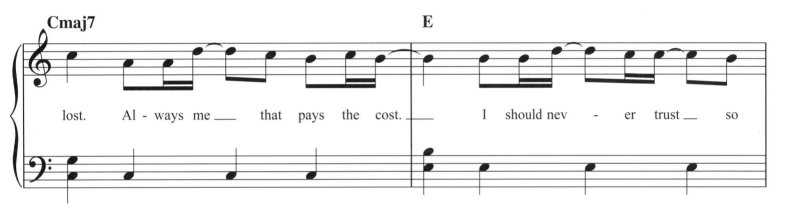

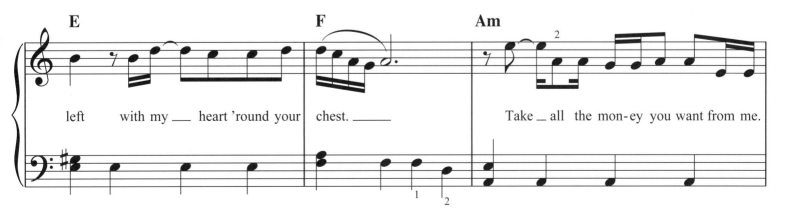

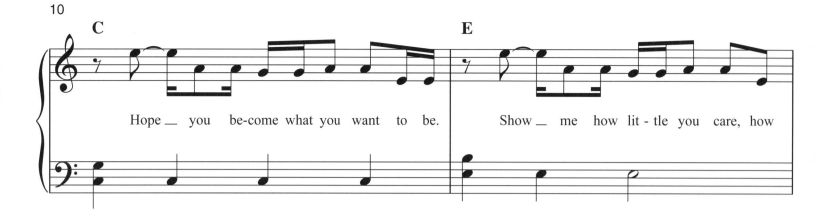

Hope — you be-come what you want to be. Show — me how lit-tle you care, how

lit-tle you care, how lit-tle you care.

knew my dia-monds leave with

you. Whoa, oh, _____ whoa, oh. _____ Al-ways knew my dia-monds leave with

knew. You're nev-er gon-na hear my heart break, _ nev-er gon-na move in

fool me.____ When you're not here I can breathe.__ Think I al-ways knew ____ my dia-monds leave with

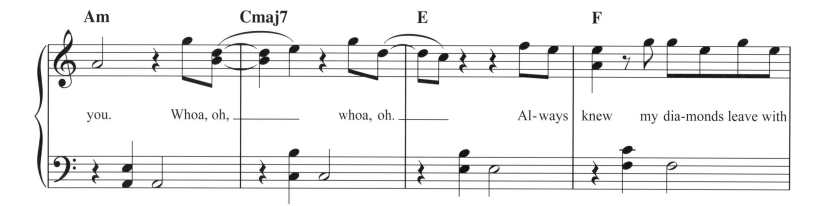

you. Whoa, oh, ____ whoa, oh. ____ Al-ways knew my dia-monds leave with

you. ____ Whoa, oh, ____ whoa, oh. ____ Al - ways

knew my dia-monds leave with you.

LIKE I CAN

Words and Music by SAM SMITH
and MATT PRIME

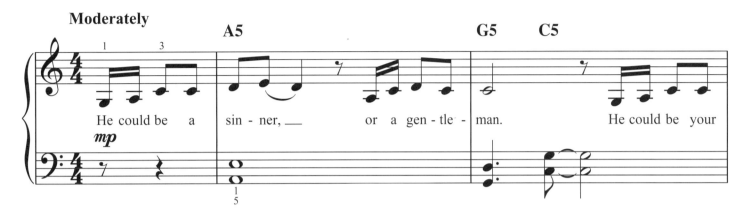

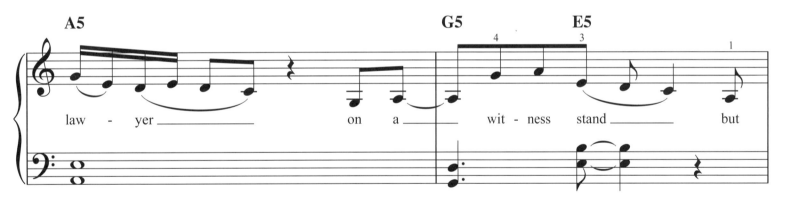

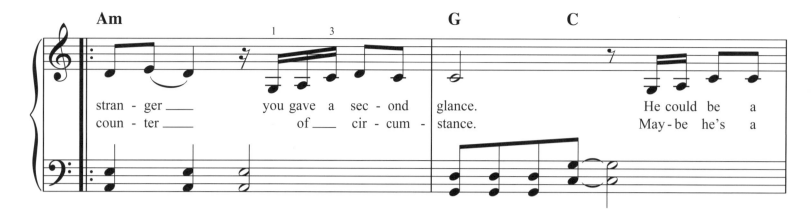

Why are you look-ing ___ down all the wrong roads? ___ When mine is the heart and the

salt of the soul. _____ There may be lov-ers ___ who hold out their hands, ___ but

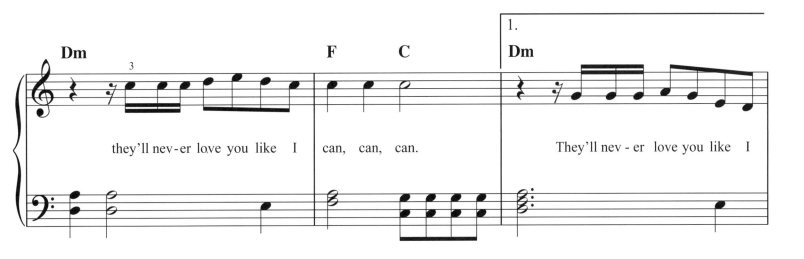

they'll nev-er love you like I can, can, can. They'll nev-er love you like I

can, can. A chance en- They'll nev-er love you like I can, can, can.

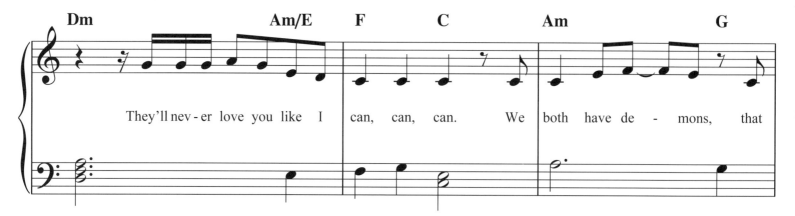

all the wrong roads? ___ When mine is the heart and the

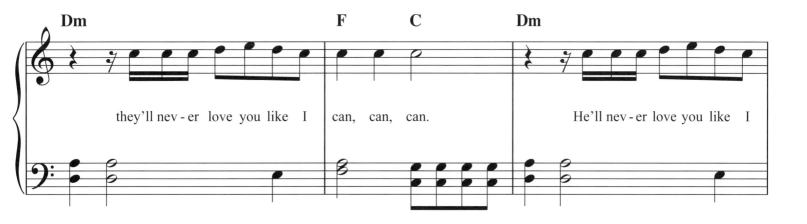

salt of the soul. ___ There may be lov-ers ___ who hold out their hands, _ but

they'll nev-er love you like I can, can, can. He'll nev-er love you like I

can, can, can. *mp* He'll nev-er love you like I can, can, can.
rit.

HOW DO YOU SLEEP?

Words and Music by SAM SMITH,
MAX MARTIN, SAVAN KOTECHA
and ILYA SALMANZADEH

Pop Ballad

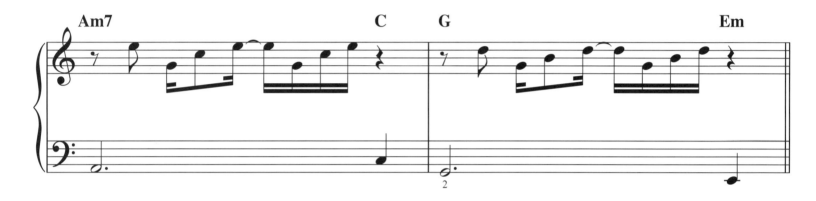

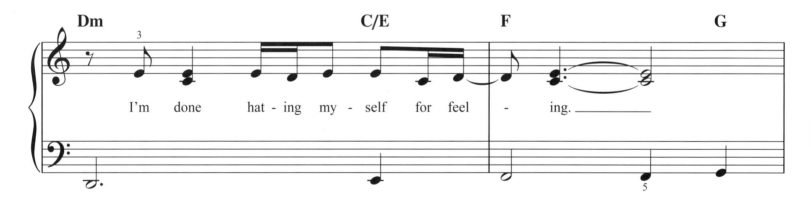

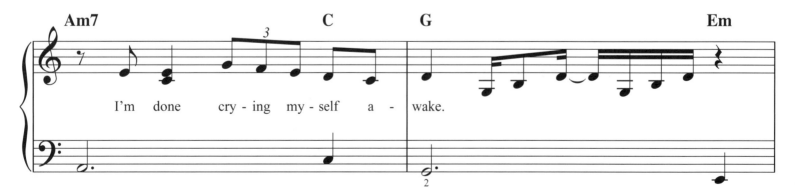

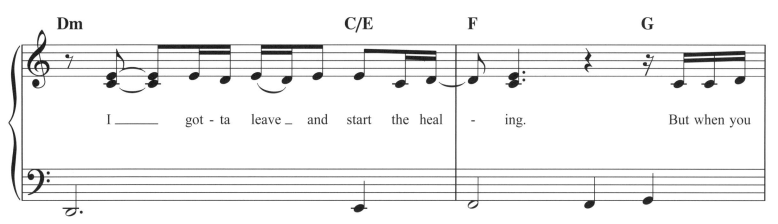

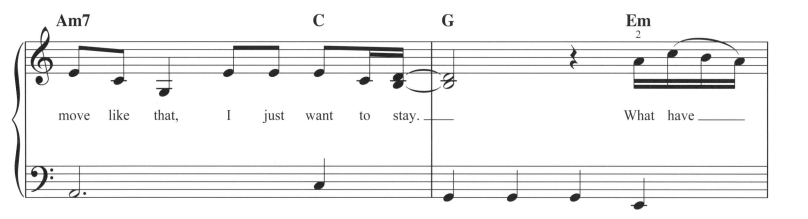

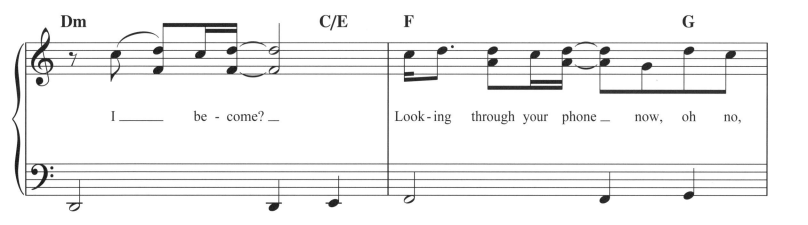

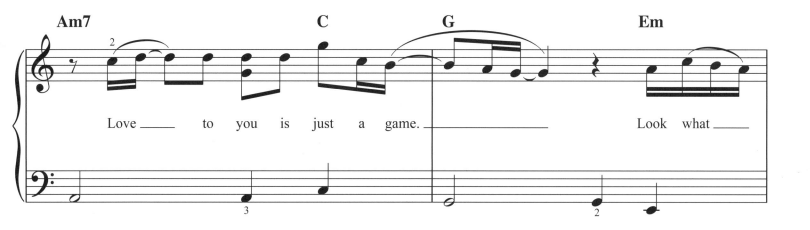

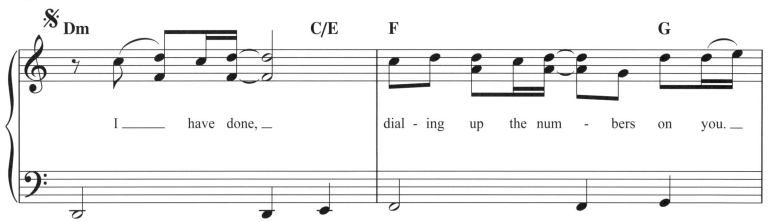

I _____ have done, _____ dial - ing up the num - bers on you. _____

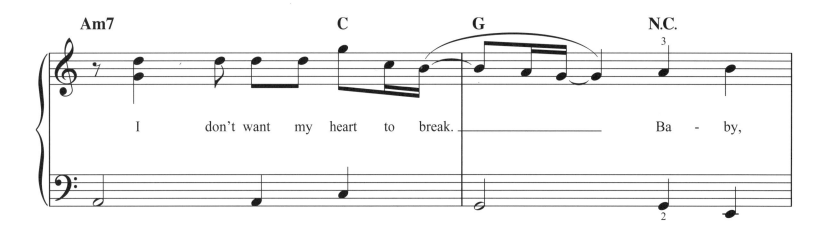

I don't want my heart to break. _____ Ba - by,

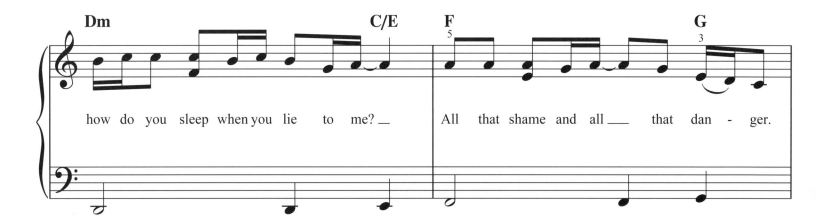

how do you sleep when you lie to me? _____ All that shame and all _____ that dan - ger.

I'm hop - ing that my love will keep you up _____ to - night. Ba - by,

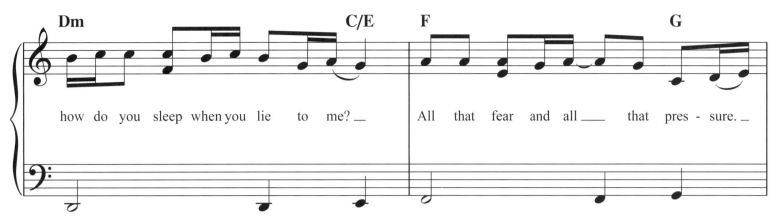

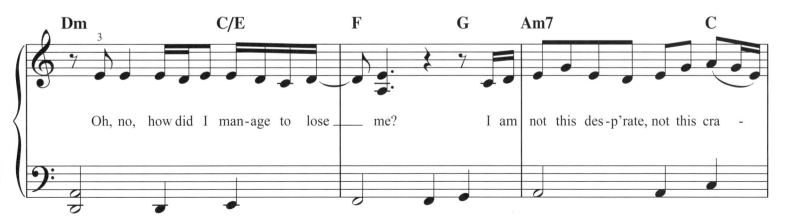

zy. ____

There's no ___ way   I'm stick-ing 'round _ to find _

____   out.

I won't lose like that,   I won't lose my - self. _

____

Look what ____

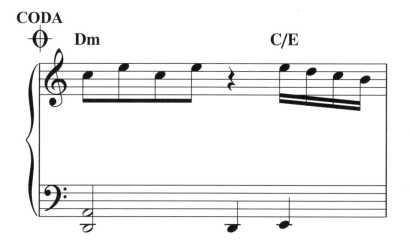

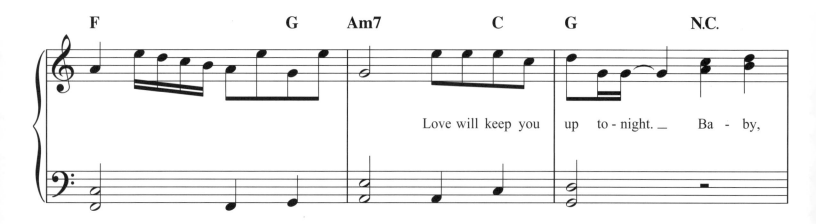

Love will keep you   up to - night. _   Ba - by,

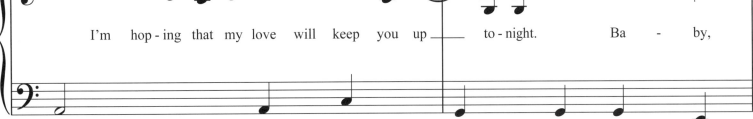

I'M NOT THE ONLY ONE

Words and Music by SAM SMITH
and JAMES NAPIER

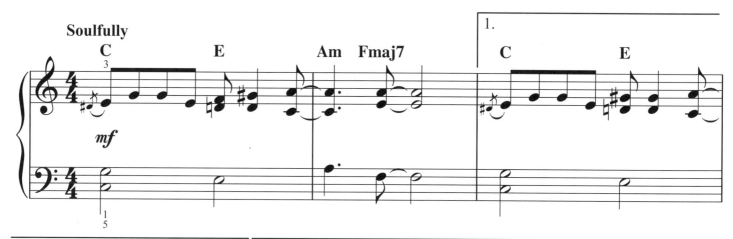

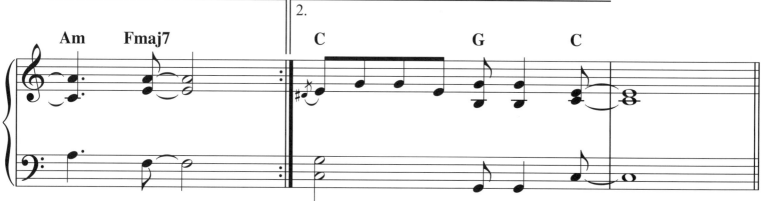

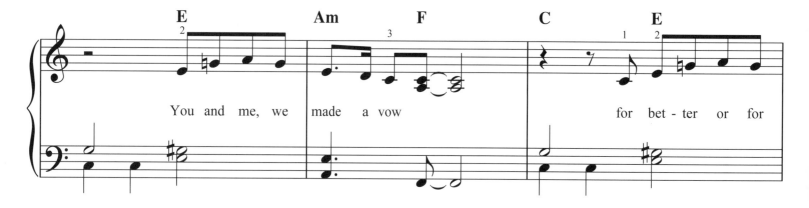

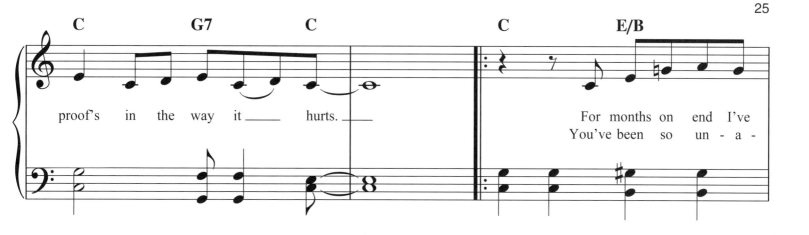

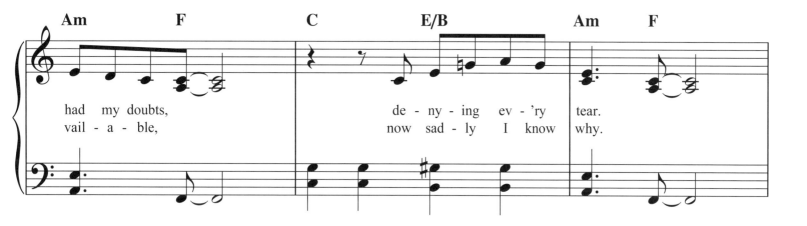

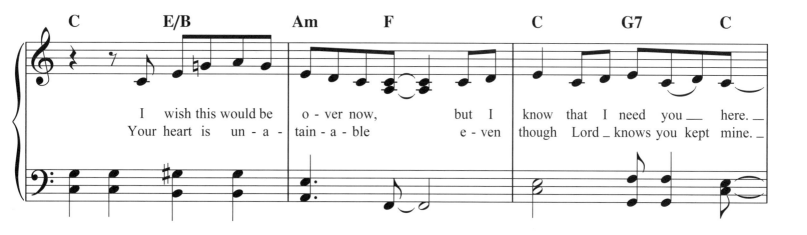

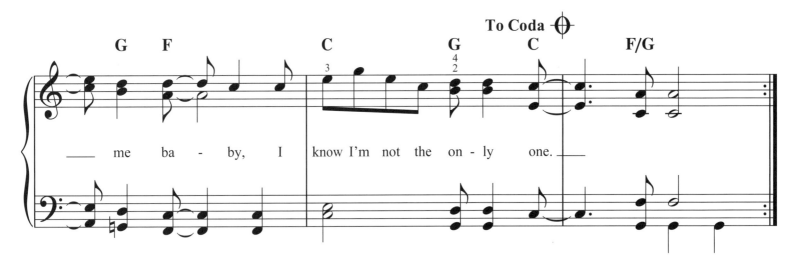

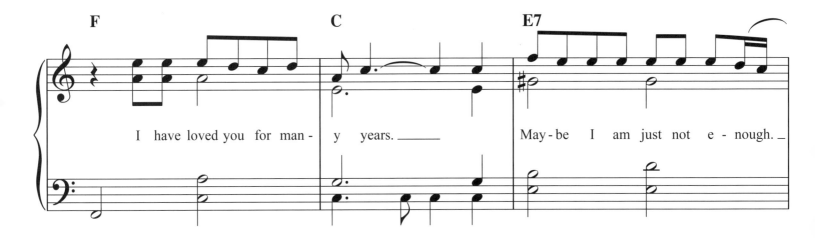

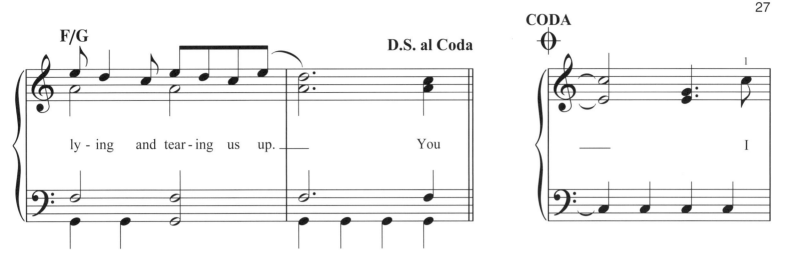

D.S. al Coda

CODA

ly - ing and tear - ing us up. ___ You

I

know I'm not the on - ly one. ___ I know I'm not the on - ly one. _

___ And I know, _ and I know, _ and I know, _ and I know, _ and I

know, _ and I know, ___ I know I'm not the on - ly one. _

LATCH

Words and Music by GUY LAWRENCE,
HOWARD LAWRENCE, JAMES NAPIER
and SAM SMITH

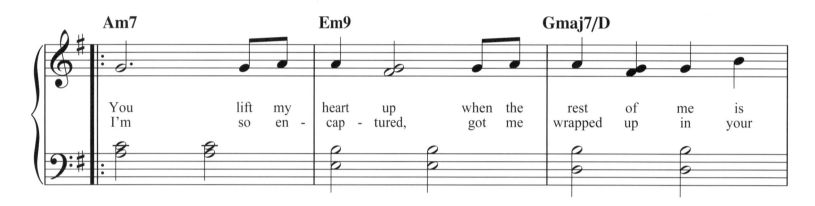

You   lift my   heart up   when the   rest of me is

I'm   so en - cap - tured,   when got me   wrapped up in your

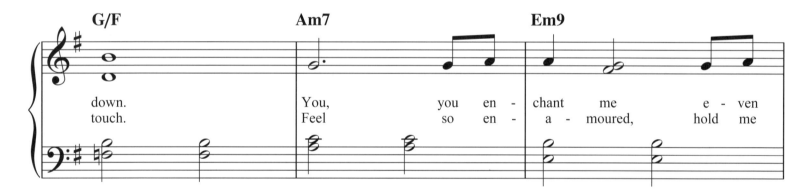

down.   You,   you en - chant me   e - ven

touch.   Feel   so en - a - moured,   hold me

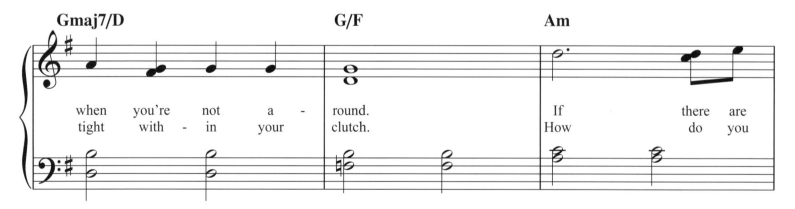

when you're not a - round.   If   there are

tight with - in your clutch.   How   do you

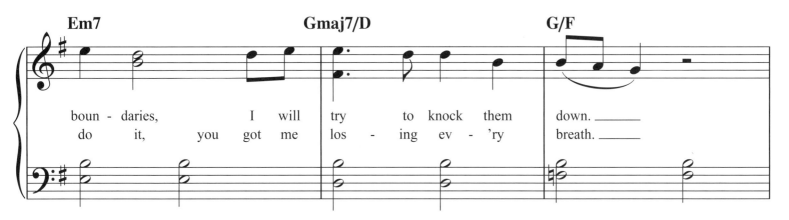

boun - daries,   I will try to knock them down. _____
do it,   you got me los - ing ev - 'ry breath. _____

I'm latch - ing on, babe. Now I know what I have
What did you give me to make my heart bleed out my

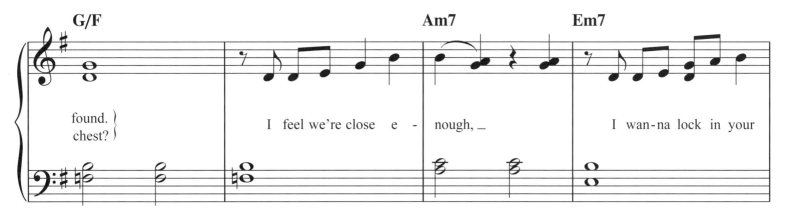

found.
chest?   I feel we're close e - nough, ___   I wan-na lock in your

love. _____   I think we're close e - nough, _____

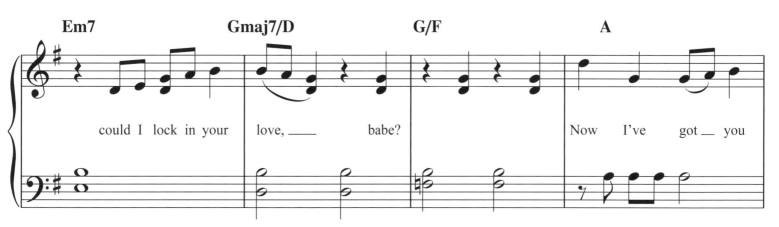

could I lock in your love, _____ babe? Now I've got _ you

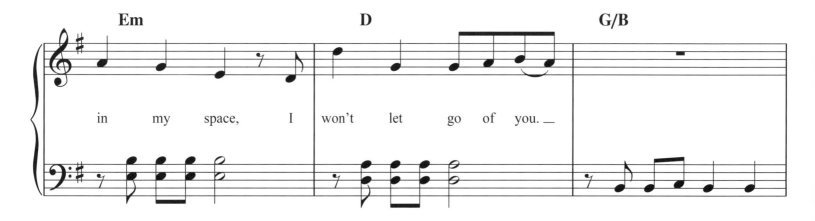

in my space, I won't let go of you. _

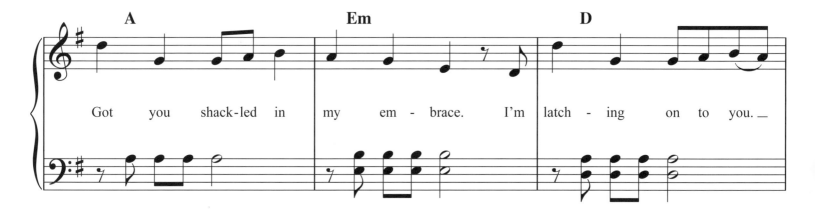

Got you shack-led in my em - brace. I'm latch - ing on to you. _

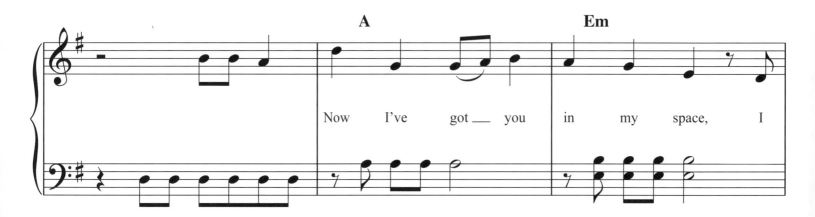

Now I've got _ you in my space, I

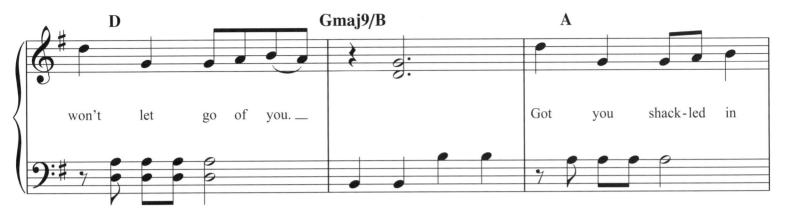

won't let go of you. ___

Got you shack-led in

my em - brace. I'm latch - ing on to you. ___

I'm latch - ing on to you. ___

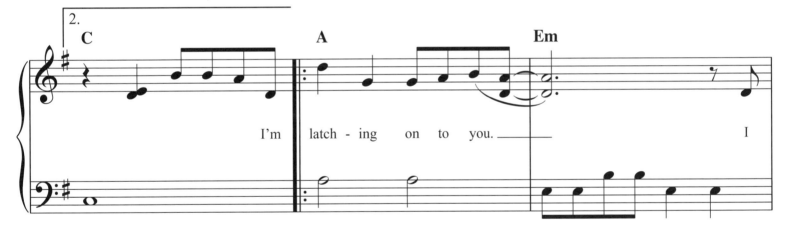

I'm latch - ing on to you. ___

I

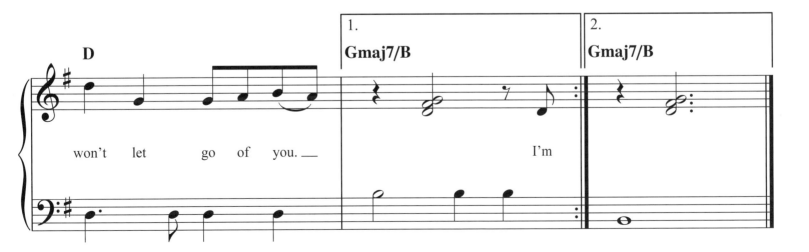

won't let go of you. ___

I'm

LAY ME DOWN

Words and Music by SAM SMITH,
JAMES NAPIER and ELVIN SMITH

Poco rubato

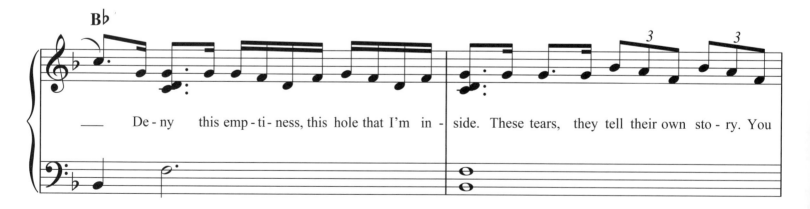

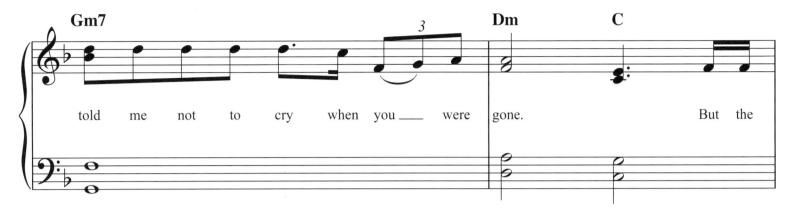

told me not to cry when you ___ were gone.   But the

feel - ing's o - ver - whelm - ing, it's much ___ too   strong. ___   Can

I lay by your ___ side? _____   Next to you, _____

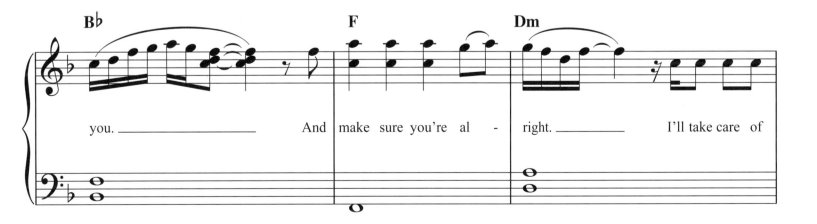

you. _____   And make sure you're al - right. _____   I'll take care of

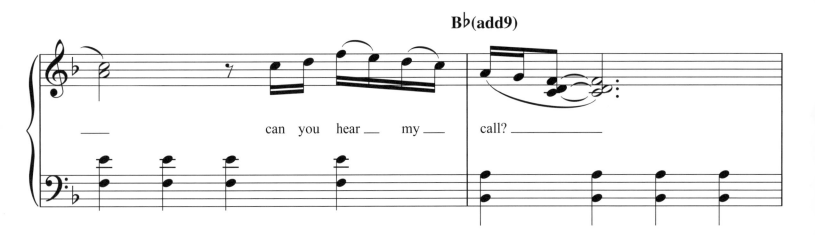

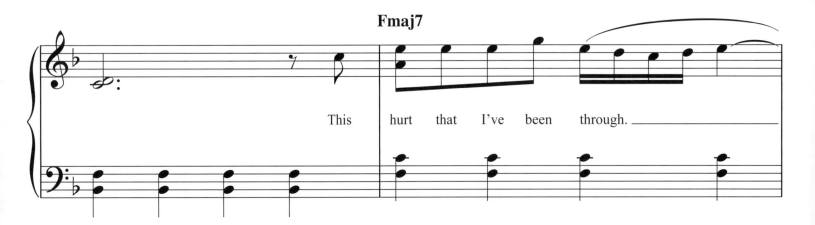

I'm miss-ing you, miss-ing you like cra - zy, oh. ____

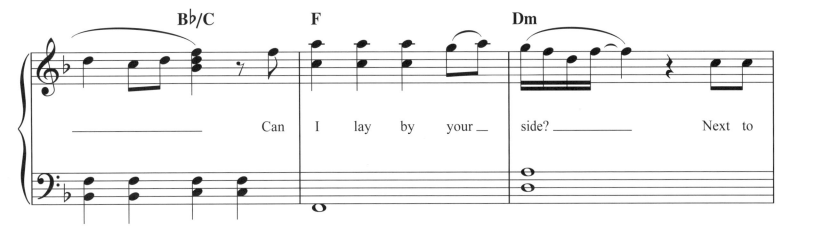

_____ Can I lay by your _ side? _____ Next to

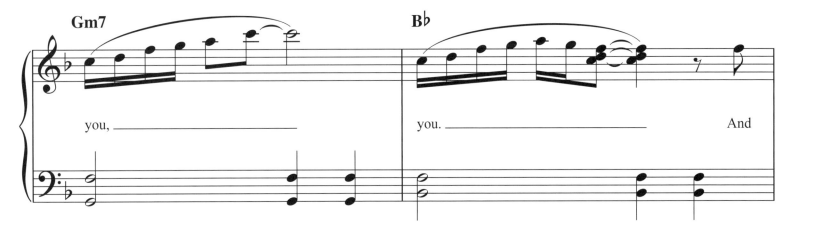

you, _____ you. _____ And

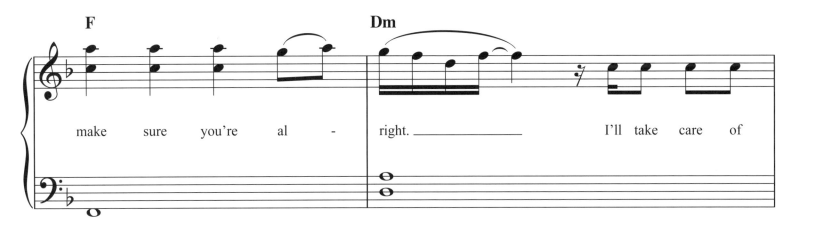

make sure you're al - right. _____ I'll take care of

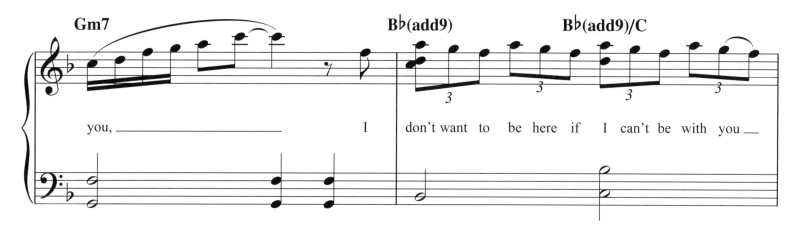

you, _____ I don't want to be here if I can't be with you __

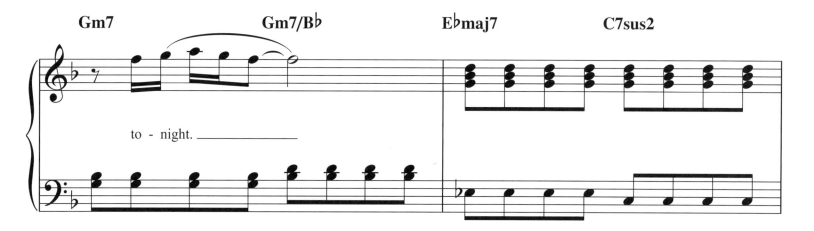

to - night. _____

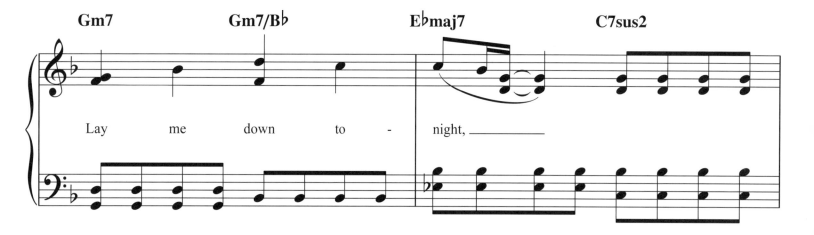

Lay me down to - night, _____

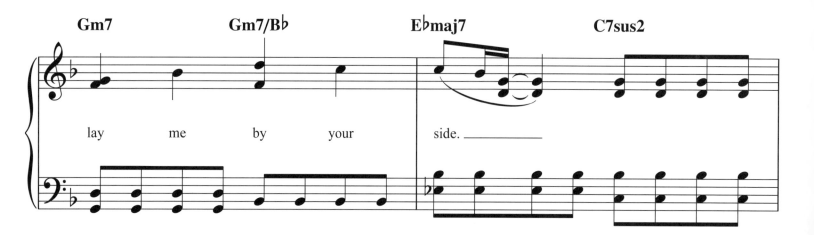

lay me by your side. _____

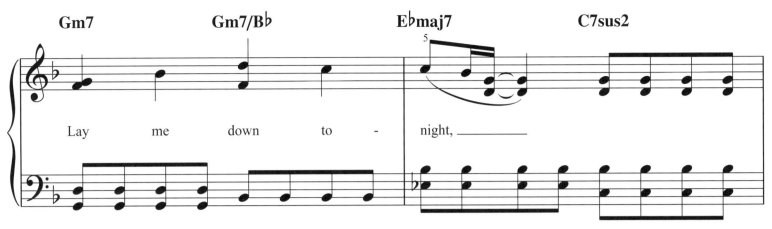

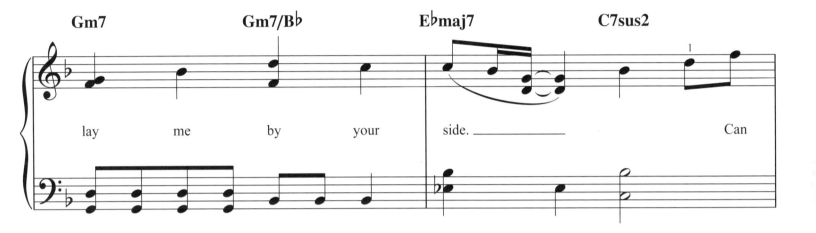

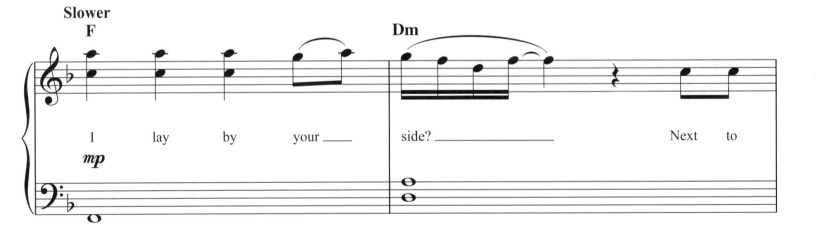

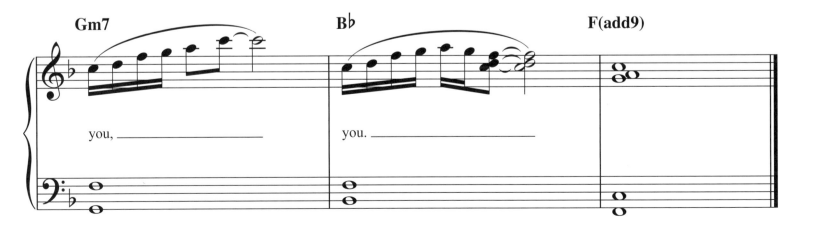

MY OASIS

Words and Music by SAM SMITH,
JAMES NAPIER and DAMINI OGULU

Moderately slow, in 2

Keep

think-ing that I'm see-ing wa - ter.   You're play-ing   tricks   on   me   in   the   sun. ___

___   See   your   shad - ow   in   the   court - yard,

but there's noth-ing I can do when it comes to you. You play

Am　　　　　　　　　　**G**

with my e - mo-tions, I'm flow - ing like the o - cean. I pray

F(add2)

for your de - vo - tion. 'Cause there's noth-ing I can do when it

Am

comes to you. My o - a, my o - a, my o - a - sis.

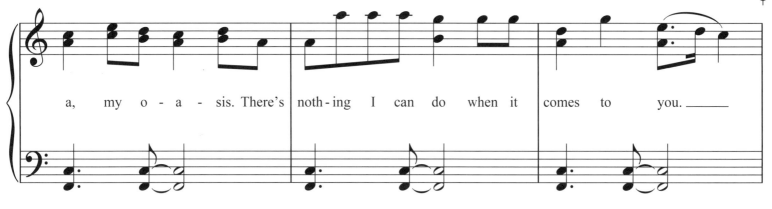

a, my o - a - sis. My o - a, my o - a, my o - a - sis. There's

noth - ing I can do when it comes to you. _____

PRAY

Words and Music by SAM SMITH,
JAMES NAPIER, TIM MOSLEY,
JOSÉ VELASQUEZ and LARRANCE DOPSON

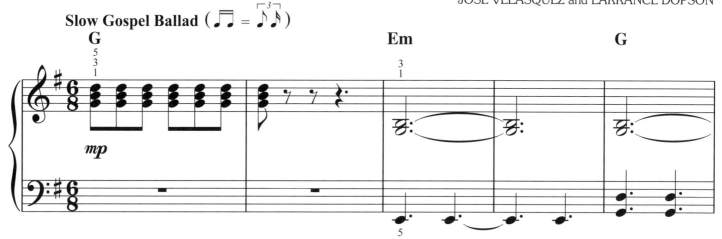

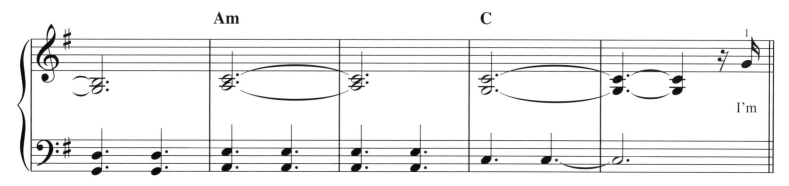

young and I'm fool-ish, I've made bad de-ci-sions. I block out the news, turn my

back on re-li-gion. Don't have no de-gree, I'm some-what na-ive. I have

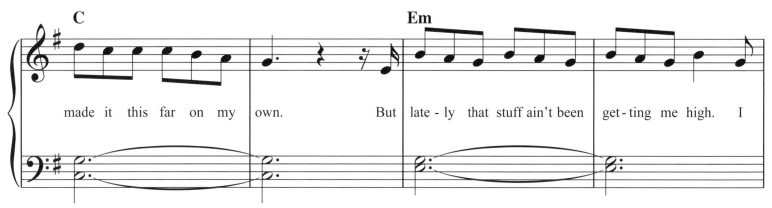

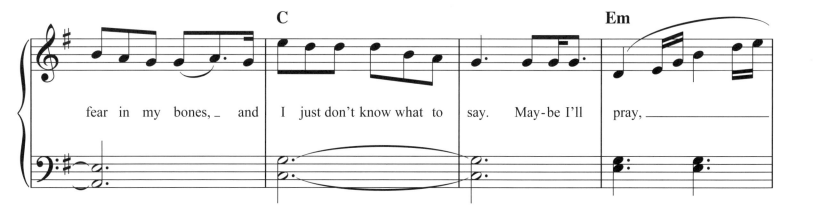

I have nev-er be-lieved in you, no, but I'm gon-na pray.

You won't find me in church,

read-ing the Bi — ble. I am still here and I'm still your dis - ci - ple. I'm down on my knees, I'm

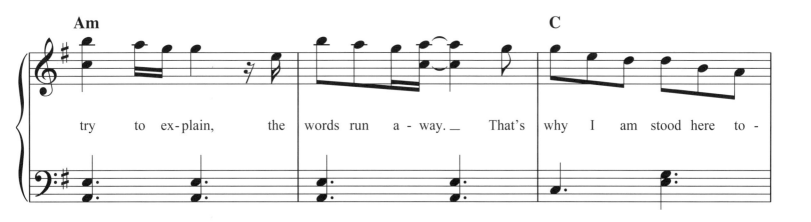

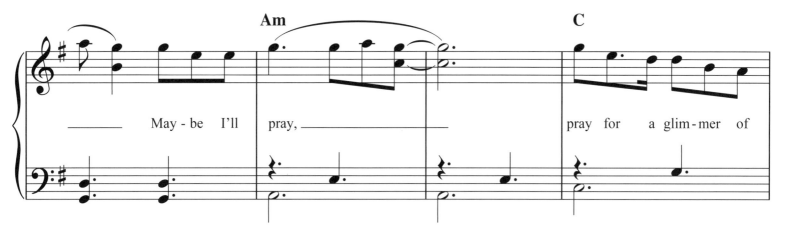

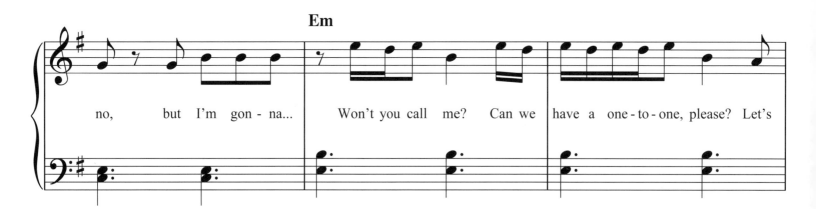

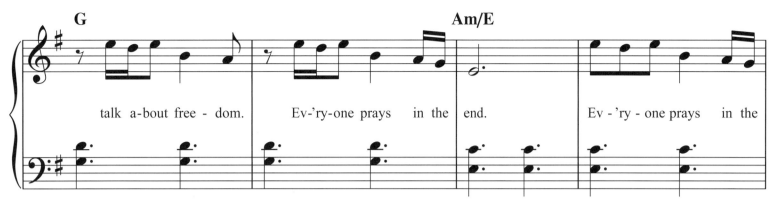

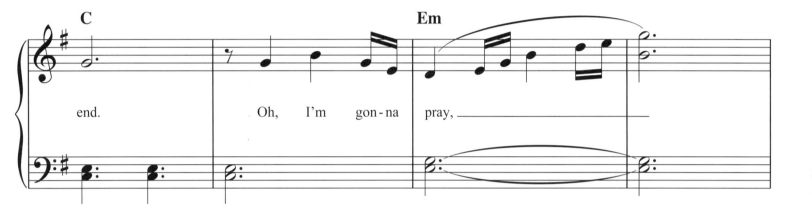

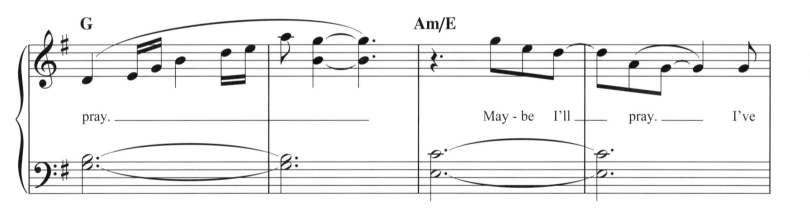

STAY WITH ME

Words and Music by SAM SMITH,
JAMES NAPIER, WILLIAM EDWARD PHILLIPS,
TOM PETTY and JEFF LYNNE

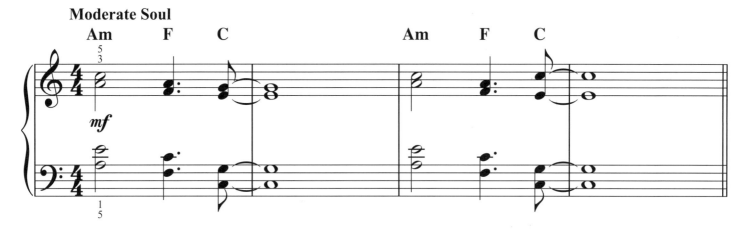

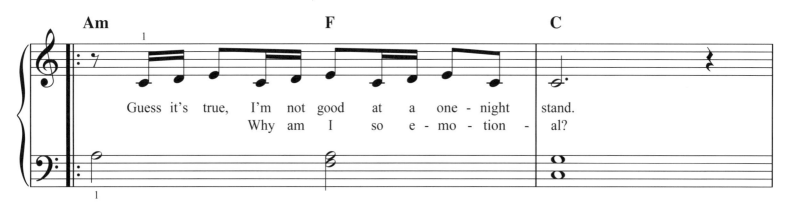

Guess it's true, I'm not good at a one - night stand.
Why am I so e - mo - tion - al?

But I still need love 'cause I'm just a man.
No, it's not a good look. Gain some self - con - trol.

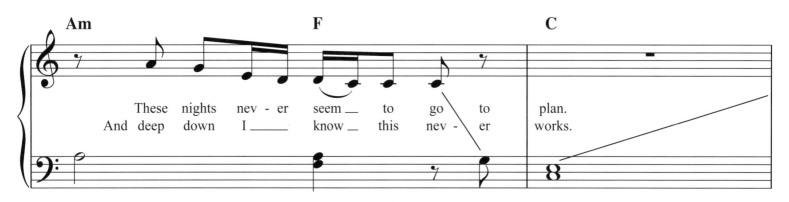

These nights nev - er seem ___ to go to plan.
And deep down I ___ know ___ this nev - er works.

I don't want you to leave, will you hold my hand?)
But you can lay with me so it does-n't hurt.)

Oh, won't you

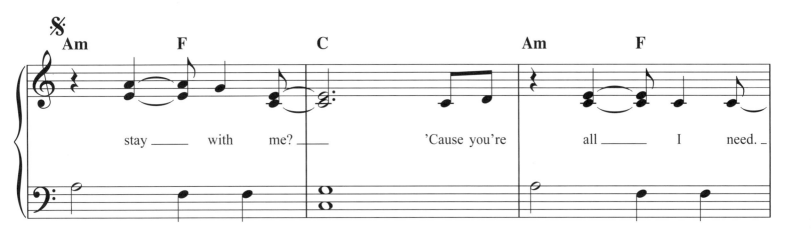

stay with me? 'Cause you're all I need.

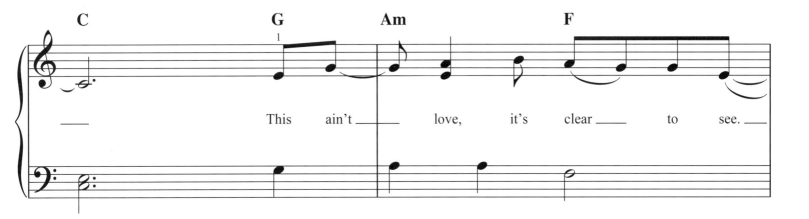

This ain't love, it's clear to see.

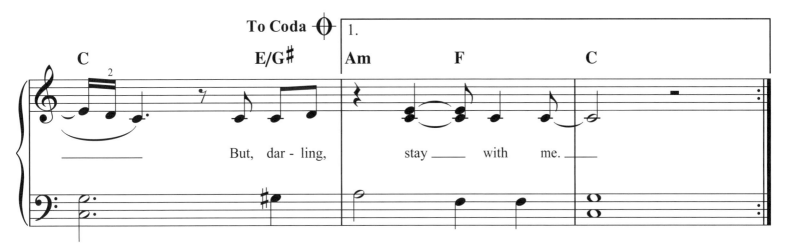

To Coda ⊕

But, dar-ling, stay with me.

52

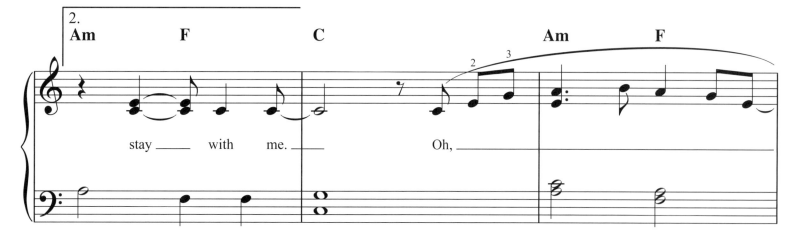

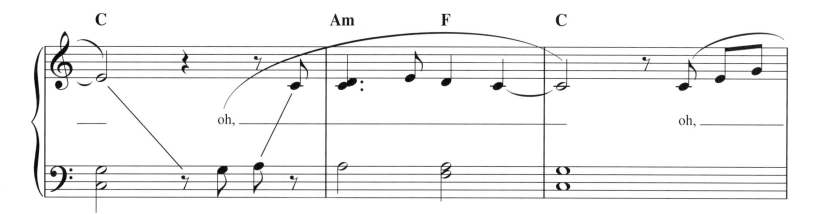

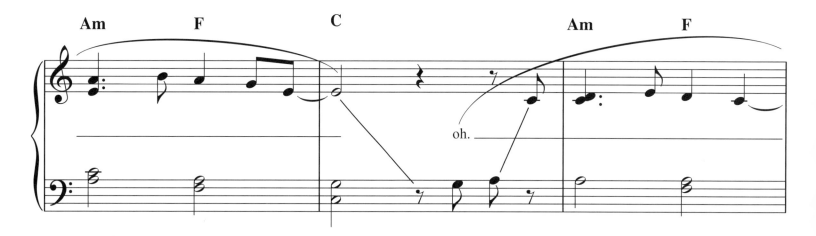

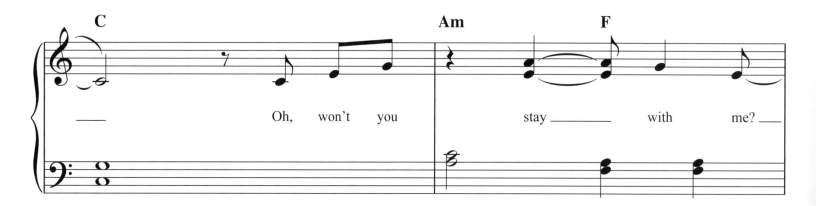

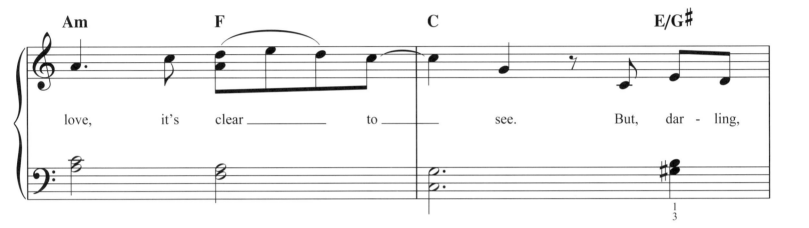

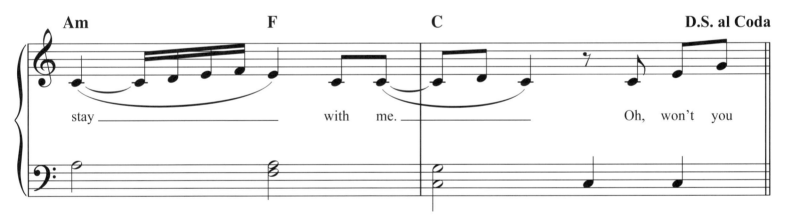

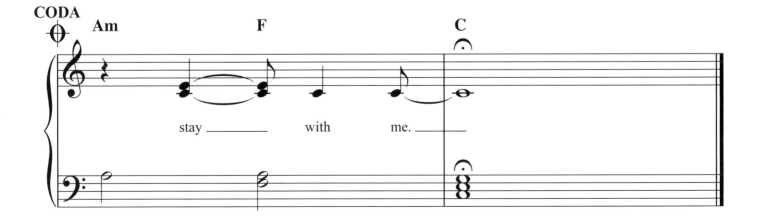

TOO GOOD AT GOODBYES

Words and Music by SAM SMITH,
TOR HERMANSEN, MIKKEL ERIKSEN
and JAMES NAPIER

Pop Ballad

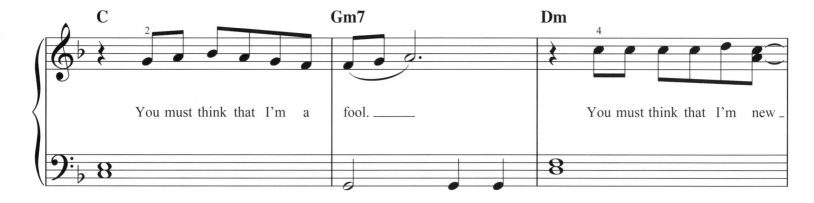

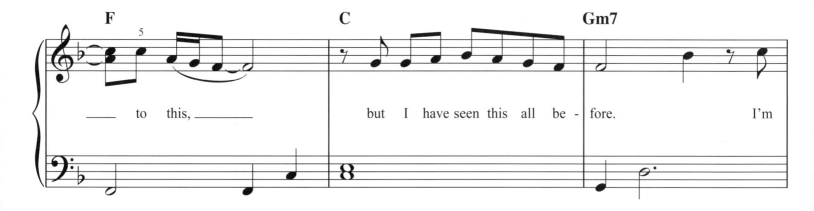

never-gon-na let you close to me, e-ven though you mean the most to me. 'Cause

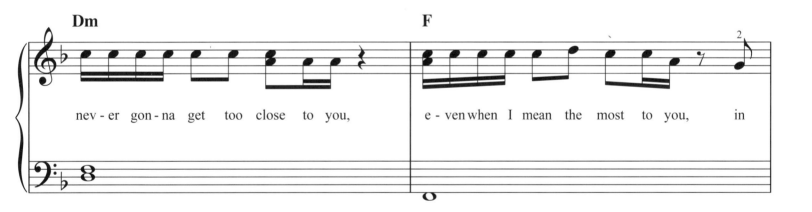

ev-'ry time I o-pen up, it hurts. _____ So I'm

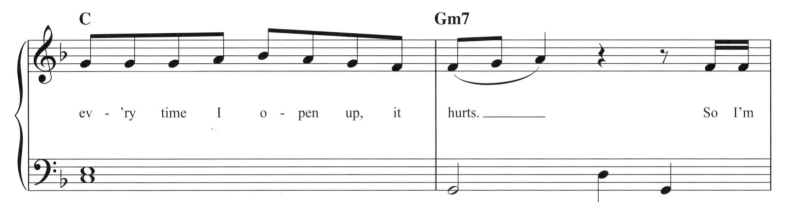

nev-er gon-na get too close to you, e-ven when I mean the most to you, in

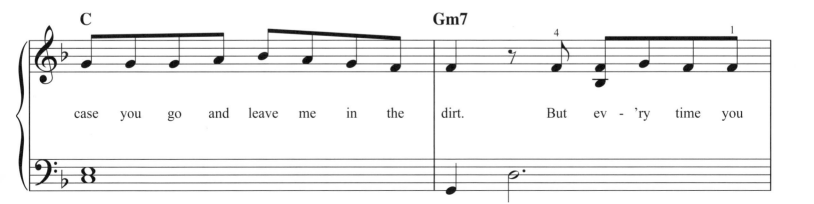

case you go and leave me in the dirt. But ev-'ry time you

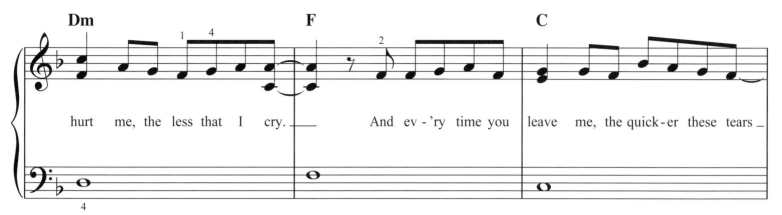

hurt me, the less that I cry. ___ And ev - 'ry time you leave me, the quick-er these tears ___

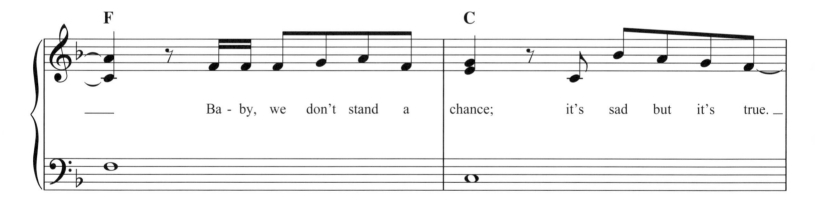

___ dry. And ev - 'ry time you walk out, the less I love you. ___

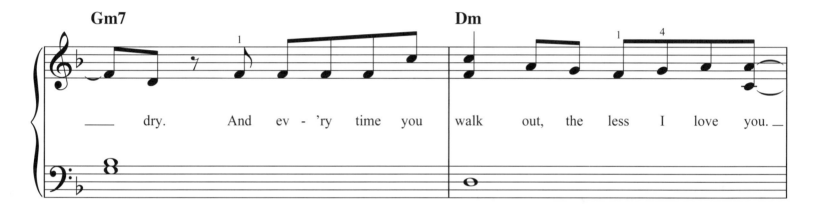

___ Ba - by, we don't stand a chance; it's sad but it's true. ___

___ I'm way too good at good - byes. ___ (I'm way too good at good - byes.)

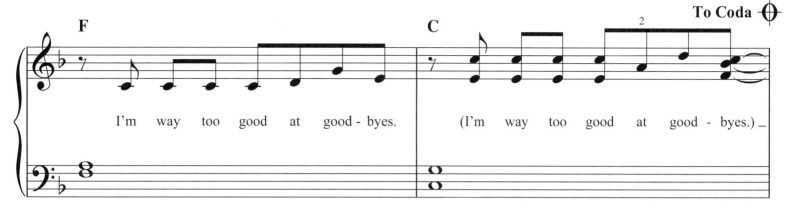

To Coda ⊕

I'm way too good at good - byes.

(I'm way too good at good - byes.) _

I know you're think - ing I'm heart - less.

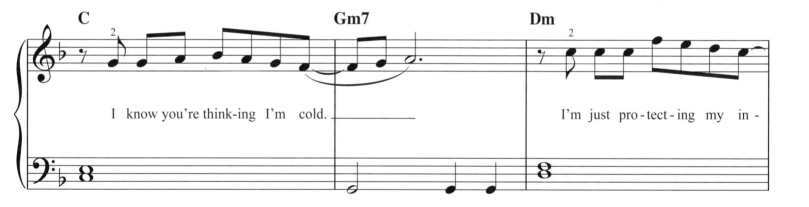

I know you're think-ing I'm cold. _____

I'm just pro-tect-ing my in-

D.S. al Coda

- no - cence. _____

I'm just pro-tect-ing my soul. _____

I'm

CODA

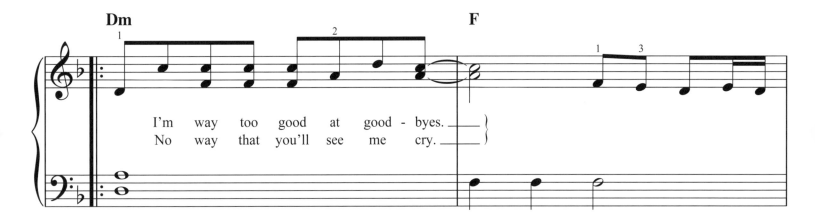

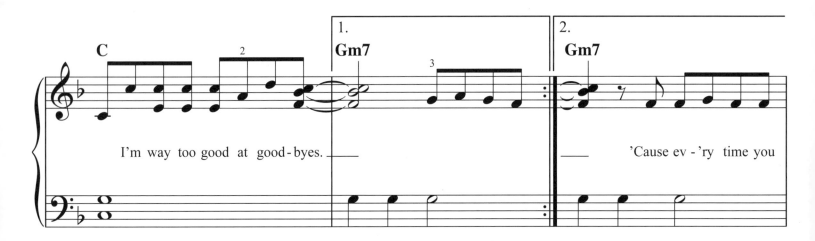

59

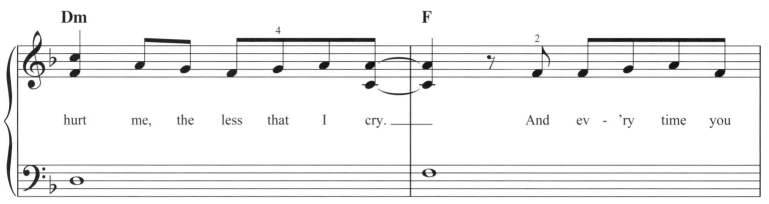

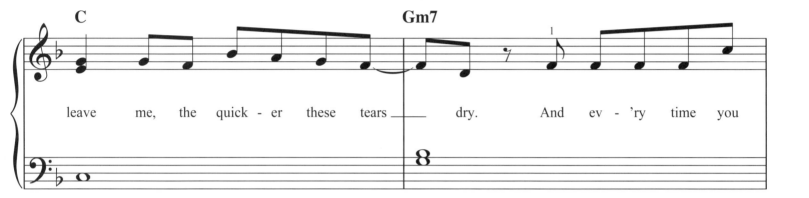

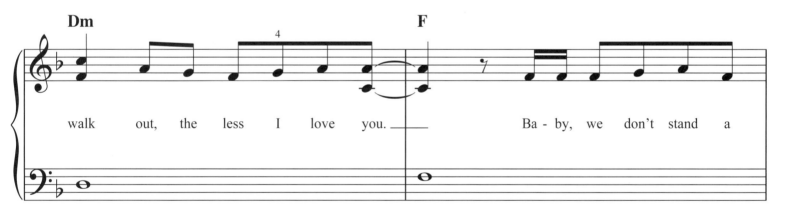

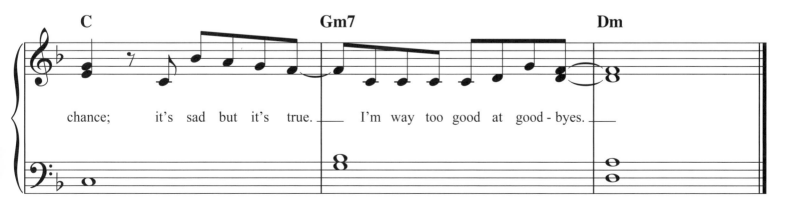

WRITING'S ON THE WALL

from SPECTRE

Words and Music by SAM SMITH
and JAMES NAPIER

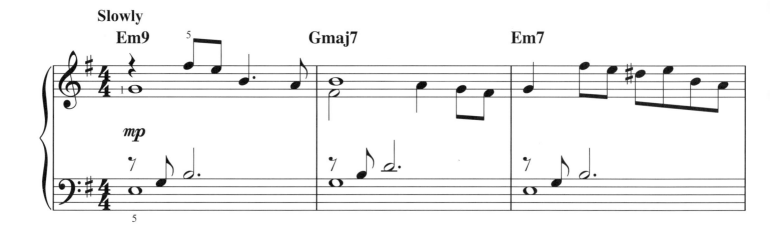

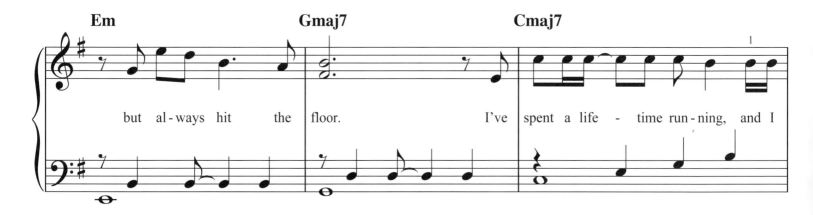

al-ways get a-way. __ But with you, I'm feel-ing some - thing that makes me want to stay. __

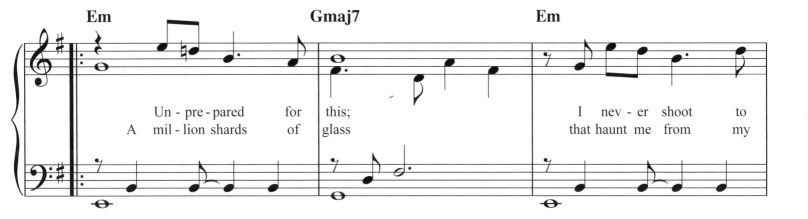

Un - pre - pared for this;
A mil - lion shards of glass

I nev - er shoot to
that haunt me from my

miss.
past.

But I feel like a storm is com - ing if I'm
As the stars be - gin to gath - er, and the

gon - na make it through the day. __ And there's no more use in run-ning, this is
light __ be - gins to fade, __ when all hope be - gins to shat-ter, know that

some-thing I've got - ta face. __

I ____ will be a - fraid. __

If I risk it all, ____

could you break our fall?

How could I

live? How do I breathe? When you're not here, I'm suf - fo - cat - ing. I wan - na feel

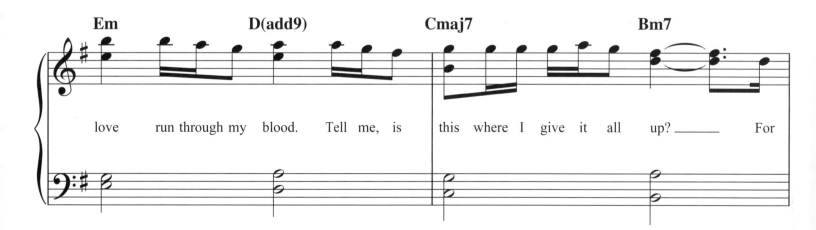

love run through my blood. Tell me, is this where I give it all up? ____ For

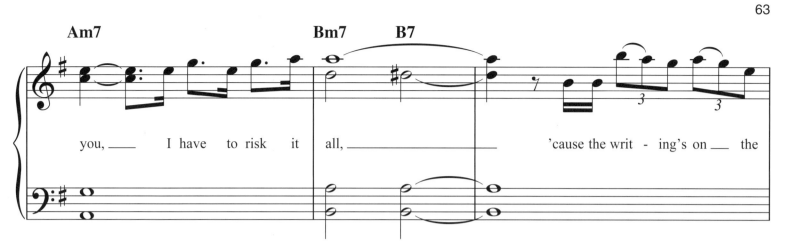

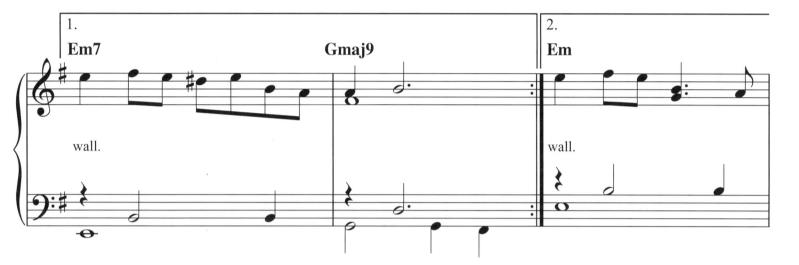

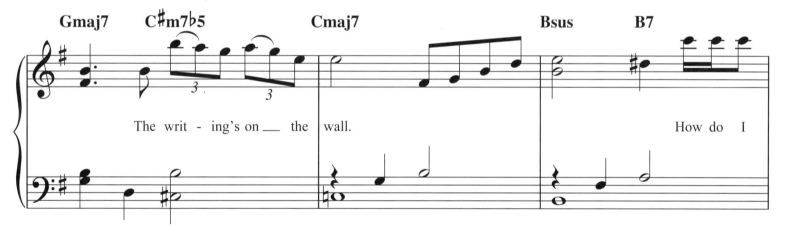

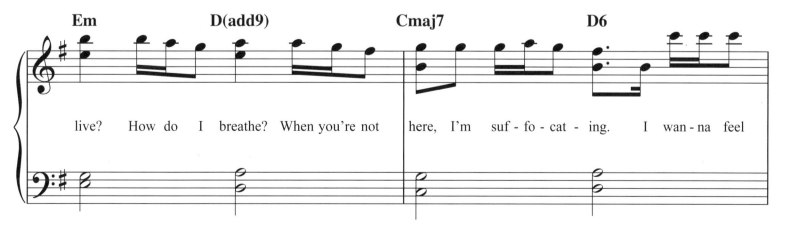

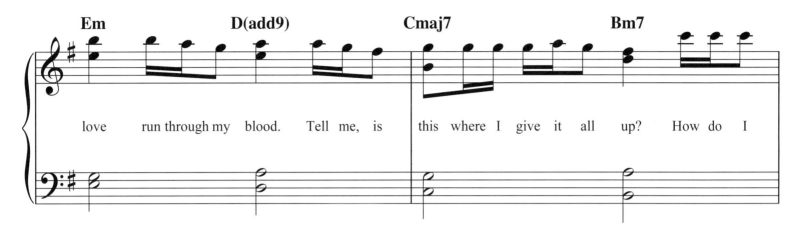